EMPATHIC EDGE

MASTERING EMPATHY FOR AUTHENTIC LEADERSHIP

DENTON GRAHAM

TABLE OF CONTENTS

Introduction v

Chapter 1: The Empathy Awakening: How Time With Family Transformed My Life...1

Chapter 2: The Heart Of Leadership: Understanding Empathy 5

Chapter 3: The Human Capital: Nurturing The Workforce.............................17

Chapter 4: Leading By Example: Personal Stories Of Empathy In Action......29

Chapter 5: From Boardroom To Home: Extending Empathy Beyond The Office...33

Chapter 6: Balancing Act: Integrating Work And Family Life.......................39

Chapter 7: The Ripple Effect: Empathy As A Catalyst For Change..............57

Chapter 8: The Journey Ahead: Embracing Continuous Improvement........63

Conclusion 69

Acknowledgments..70

INTRODUCTION

Empathy has always been an essential attribute for leaders, but it is now gaining significance and importance. Far from being a soft approach, it may provide big business results.

You've always known that displaying empathy benefits individuals, but a recent study shows that it's important for everything from invention to retention. Great leadership necessitates diverse talents to foster engagement, happiness, and performance, with empathy topping the list of what leaders must master.

What is an Empathetic Leader?

An empathic leader is concerned about their team members' well-being and lives within and outside work. These leaders want to create a loving, helpful, and understanding environment; they're there to help their team overcome obstacles and succeed.

Empathetic leaders aim to comprehend a person's situation and provide appropriate counsel and assistance. These encounters make employees feel protected and respected.

Why Empathy Matters at Work

An unempathetic workplace generates a stressful environment, reducing productivity and corporate goals. Workplace incivility is increasing, resulting in higher turnover, worse customer experiences, and lower performance. Furthermore, stressful work conditions disrupt sleep. Low sleep leads to low productivity.

Overall, empathic leadership fosters a safe and productive workplace, providing employees with the resources they need to succeed. A sympathetic attitude is unlikely to produce any negative results.

CHAPTER 1

THE EMPATHY AWAKENING:
HOW TIME WITH FAMILY
TRANSFORMED MY LIFE

For much of my life, I was driven by a relentless pursuit of excellence in my work. After working in retail leadership for more than 20 years, consistency in the way I show up at work and helping others grow has always been my passion. Achievements, accolades, and occupational awards provided me with a sense of accomplishment and fueled my desire to be recognized for my contributions. This drive intensified after the birth of my daughter, as I focused on providing for my family, working even harder to garner more awards and recognition.

However, a significant turning point came when I experienced a work furlough, a pause in my career that was both unexpected and unsettling. For the first time since I was fifteen years old, I found myself with an abundance of time, a luxury I had not known in years. This period, while initially daunting, turned into an invaluable opportunity for self-reflection and connection.

During these months, I spent precious time with my now Ten-year-old daughter and reconnected deeply with my wife. This time was transformative; it allowed me to truly understand my family in a way I had not previously. I began to see beyond the roles we played in our busy lives and to appreciate the individuals they are.

This period of enforced rest gave me the space to explore my own passions and to extend empathy toward myself—a crucial but often overlooked aspect of personal growth. I came to understand that the quality of time I spend with my family is the true measure of success, far surpassing any professional accolades.

Through this empathetic awakening, I realized that my relentless pursuit of work excellence was driven by a desire to provide for my family, but the true value lay in being present with them. This shift in perspective has been life-changing. I am now dedicated to ensuring that the time I spend with my family is meaningful and that I approach all aspects of my life with empathy.

This chapter marks the beginning of our journey into the heart of empathy, illustrating how it can transform not only our professional lives but also the relationships that matter most. By sharing this personal story, I hope to highlight the profound impact that empathy can have when extended beyond the workplace and into the very fabric of our personal lives.

DENTON GRAHAM

CHAPTER 2

THE HEART OF LEADERSHIP:
UNDERSTANDING EMPATHY

Empathy is like a universal solvent. Any challenge submerged in empathy becomes solvable. Understanding others' emotions is an important ability in the business. It may help us settle problems, create more productive teams, and strengthen our connections with coworkers, clients, and customers.

However, while most of us are competent in learning new technical abilities, we may feel unprepared to improve our interpersonal skills. Many individuals are uncomfortable sharing their own sentiments, let alone those of others!

What Is Empathy?

In its most basic form, empathy is the capacity to identify emotions in others and grasp their points of view on a topic. Empathy, when fully developed, allows you to use that understanding to lift someone else's spirits and help them through difficult times.

Empathy is sometimes mistaken with sympathy, although the two are not the same. Sympathy is a feeling of care for someone and a wish that they could be happier. Unlike empathy, sympathy does not entail a shared viewpoint or emotions.

You can feel pity for someone in tears on the street, for example, even if you have no idea what their situation is. Sympathy can lead to empathy, although it does not always. Empathy is one of five essential components of emotional intelligence, a critical leadership talent. It progresses through three stages: cognitive empathy, emotional empathy, and compassionate empathy.

Cognitive Empathy

Cognitive empathy is the ability to understand another person's thoughts or feelings. The spectator doesn't need to be emotionally engaged.

Managers may find cognitive empathy valuable in knowing how their team members are feeling and hence what leadership style will best suit them today. Similarly, sales executives may use it to gauge a customer's mood, allowing them to adopt the most appropriate tone for a conversation.

The ability to be cognitively empathetic is primarily cerebral, emotionally indifferent, and logical. This indicates that some individuals make bad use of it. People who possess a Machiavellian personality characteristic, for instance, could employ cognitive empathy to take advantage of emotionally weak individuals.

Emotional Empathy

The capacity to empathize with another person emotionally allows one to have a greater understanding of that individual. Because it alters or affects you, it is also called "affective empathy." It takes more than just understanding someone else's emotions to have a sincere connection with them.

This level of empathy might be too much for some of us. Strong empathy inclinations can cause a person to lose themselves in the difficulties or suffering of others, which can occasionally be detrimental to their emotional health. This is especially true if they think they need help to handle the circumstance.

By taking pauses, examining your boundaries, and improving your capacity to handle such a demanding position, you may prevent this type of emotional generosity burnout.

It is beneficial for any team leader to have at least a minimal level of emotional empathy. It fosters honesty and transparency as well as the development of trust between managers and team members. However, empathy is most useful when it is paired with action.

Compassionate Empathy

The most active type of empathy is compassionate empathy. It entails experiencing another person's emotional suffering and showing care for them, but it also entails acting practically to lessen it.

Consider the scenario when a member of your team is furious and frustrated because they made a mistake while delivering a crucial presentation. It's important to acknowledge their pain, and it's even more important to validate their response by exhibiting same emotions yourself. The best thing to do is to set out some time for them and provide them with advice or practical help so they can handle the issue and get ready for the next one.

Importance Of Building Trust

You have trust. It is the cornerstone of each healthy partnership. You have faith that the fruit in your preferred supermarket will be delicious and fresh. You have faith that every Starbucks you visit will serve you the same pumpkin spice latte. You have faith that your barber won't give you a mohawk even if all you've requested is a trim. What occurs then if that trust is betrayed? It jeopardizes and ends the relationship.

The Importance of Trust in Leadership

At work, the same dynamic exists. If you've made the correct hiring decisions, you have faith that your staff members are competent and giving their all. However, are you aware of your workers' level of trust? Many leaders don't think trust is important or haven't given it any attention (assuming trust flows both ways). Sadly, nothing could be farther from the reality than that. Additionally, you will only be a very good leader if you work to gain and maintain the trust of your team members.

Why Is Trust Important in the Workplace

In the workplace, trust is essential for several reasons. Employee confidence in leaders and other employees encourages moral decision-making, loyalty, and a greater desire to stick with a company. Another important factor in lowering tension and animosity at work is trust. Furthermore, trust aids in overcoming aversion to change. A positive and effective work environment depends on the growth and maintenance of trust.

Trust Flows Through Power

The cornerstone of excellent leadership is trust. According to a study, one of the most significant bases of power when managing employees is referent power, which is predicated on the idea that an individual exhibits behaviors and qualities that win the respect and trust of others. Building trust offers you the ability to accomplish goals. Employees are more likely to follow your leadership when they have faith in you, particularly when it comes to handling unknown or unclear situations.

Trust is the Opposite of Fear

Fear, disengagement, lack of commitment, lower returns on investment, and decreased productivity are all bred by mistrust. Team performance will suffer in the absence of trust since it is essential for efficient operation. Workers will struggle to make choices or own up to their errors because they worry about the consequences of doing so. However, when you've built trust, employees may ask for help and assistance without feeling afraid to do so.

Trust Leads to Breakthroughs

Your staff members will feel free to voice their thoughts and opinions, even if they don't align with your own if you are a trustworthy leader. Employees who don't mind speaking out will expose you to various viewpoints and may suggest fresh concepts or fixes. Furthermore, people are more inclined to alter their behavior under management with whom they have developed trust. Consequently, trust is crucial when attempting to put changes into practice and raise employee performance.

Trust Helps with Damage Control

In a fear-filled workplace, staff members tend to hold off on admitting faults, which frequently results in more issues than if they had spoken out sooner. When working in a trustworthy atmosphere, staff members aren't scared to accept responsibility for their errors and provide remedies. This lessens the consequences of a mistake and makes it easier for the staff member to see the incident as a teaching moment.

Trust Creates Future Leaders

Trust gives your staff the confidence to take responsibility for their achievement. They may overcome obstacles more effectively, accept accountability for their actions and outcomes, and develop their leadership abilities when they own their achievements. Capable leaders nurture other leaders, and infectious leadership spreads like wildfire.

How Empathy Fuels Effective Communication and Problem-Solving

The public no longer views companies as mere profit-making entities. They hold them in high regard as a brand and see them as community members.

Both consumers and staff choose companies according to their behaviors and principles. A company's reputation and finances will suffer if its employees, who are the main contributors to its success, are not heard and their concerns are not addressed. Empathy communication is one technique that creates a compassionate workplace and enhances connections between employers and employees and between businesses and customers.

What is empathy in communication?

Empathy is the capacity to comprehend and experience another person's emotions in communication. It entails paying attention to what your audience is saying, expressing empathy for their feelings, and reacting to demonstrate your concern for them as people.

Empathic communication may help small businesses establish deep bonds with their clients and staff and promote loyalty and trust, all of which will ultimately increase sales.

Why is empathy important for effective communication?

Lack of empathy in communication can result in disagreements, snap judgments, and diminished trust. This can be equivalent in business to:

- Lost sales: Salespeople who lack empathy and companies who overlook significant civil cases risk losing their consumers' loyalty.

- Tarnished reputation: As more staff members and clients witness your company's lack of empathy, critics may begin to voice their opinions about it.

- Employee turnover: Employee retention is lower when they receive indifferent treatment on a regular basis.

- Diminished productivity: Employee performance may suffer in the long run if they are unable to discuss personal matters with management.

According to a study, 59% of workers say they're scared to discuss mental health concerns with managers or HR because they think it would jeopardize their job security. But 77% of CEOs fear they may lose respect if they show too much empathy. However, if they consider the advantages for the business, they'll see that the time investment was well worth it. As an illustration, according to 70% of workers and HR experts, a business with empathy may boost worker motivation. Additional advantages include of:

- Increased morale among staff members as a result of having bosses who are attentive to their requirements.

- Enhanced mutual regard and cooperation between groups.

- Increased output and involvement because employees feel appreciated and supported.

- Increased client loyalty when people perceive your business to be compassionate (while discussing humanitarian concerns).

- Lower staff turnover.

The key takeaway is that founders should appoint sympathetic management teams to promote empathy at work. Additionally, it teaches PR staff and teams who interact with customers how to communicate empathically. Communication abilities with empathy What, then, are the necessary abilities for mastering empathic communication? Is it providing a sympathetic ear? Or is it just being polite?

Before you can communicate more empathetically, you must define empathy. Empathy isn't about trying to solve someone else's problems or expressing sympathy for them. It's about appreciating the perspective of others. It doesn't mean you have to sympathize with or agree with them; instead, try putting yourself in their position and understanding why they feel the way they do.

They use cooperation, mindfulness, and compassion to increase your capacity for empathic communication. For instance, there are several approaches to handling an employee who doesn't perform up to par. Did they have an incident outside of work that affected their capacity to complete the task at hand? If so, are they at ease enough to share it with you?

If they don't, you must improve your sympathetic communication skills and provide a welcoming environment for candid conversations. Once your employees are at ease speaking with you, look for opportunities to help them inside and outside their job descriptions. This might entail providing greater flexibility or enlisting outside assistance for further direction.

Two other skills worth honing include:

1. **Self-awareness**

   the capacity to identify and comprehend your feelings, ideas, and actions. Understanding the effects of your behavior on team dynamics and corporate culture may be greatly aided by self-awareness. For instance, consider your communication style and consider how it could affect the team. You may work toward developing empathy and more solid connections by identifying and resolving any areas that require improvement.

2. **Emotional intelligence**

   the capacity to identify, comprehend, and control your emotions and those of others. Leaders who can perceive their team members' emotions and react accordingly can enhance communication and teamwork.

How to communicate with empathy

A leader must acquire and put into practice empathy through communication. Here are some pointers for consistently talking with empathy:

Show nonverbal cues.

Words are not as loud as actions. Empathy isn't only about what you say but also how you express it. Your true thoughts may be seen through your body language. I can communicate empathy and understanding through nonverbal cues like body language and facial expressions. To demonstrate that I'm involved and sympathetic, I want to keep eye contact, nod, and make the proper facial expressions.

Making eye contact and occasionally nodding while someone is speaking demonstrates your interest and attentiveness. Additionally, you might utilize facial expressions like a worried or contemplative look to show empathy and understanding. You must first develop self-awareness toto comprehend your responses and the reasons behind them to enhance nonverbal cues. Then, discover how to rewire your emotions and mentality so that you can respond with true empathy.

Ask for clarification vs. making assumptions.

Refrain from assuming to know someone's motivations or what they intend when they say anything.Ask questions rather than assuming things to make sure the conversation is fruitful. Asking clarifying questions may help you make sure that everyone is on the same page and can also help you comprehend other people's perspectives.

For example, don't assume that a person is attempting to be lazy if they ask to work from home full-time. Find out why they decided as they did. Perhaps they have a little kid to care for and cannot afford daycare, or they have a health issue that makes driving or controlling symptoms at work challenging.

Keep an open mind vs. judging.

Try to see things from their perspective rather than discounting other people's ideas and opinions because they conflict with your own. Even if you believe that remaining at home isn't the best option, sometimes you come to work despite having a health issue. However, not everyone handles private matters in the same way, and some people want to keep their affairs private.

Internal judgment and criticism of others sometimes result in a stressful and aggressive atmosphere. Rather, approach every discussion with an open mind and a willingness to discover points of agreement with the other person.

Use assertive communication.

Being assertive in communication is expressing your ideas and feelings straightforwardly, self-assuredly, and unambiguously without coming across as hostile or submissive. It gives you the confidence to be sincere without coming across as impolite.

Constructive discourse may be fostered, and defensiveness or conflict can be avoided with assertive communication. Expressing empathy without condemnation or criticism is possible when you communicate in a forceful or nonjudgmental manner. Use "I" statements rather than critical or accusing "you" comments to convey your thoughts and viewpoints. You may say something like, "I'm concerned about the missed deadlines and how they impact the project," instead of, "You're not meeting your deadlines."

Practice active listening and patience.

Many people need help listening during a quarrel to respond. Give the other person space to talk and practice patience to foster more empathic communication. Make sure you comprehend what they're saying by actively listening to them at the same time. Develop your self-awareness to recognize when you are thinking of responses and defenses rather than listening to what is being said. To concentrate on the other person, mentally note the situation and "turn off" your thoughts.

Several pointers to enhance attentive listening:

- Make eye contact

- If there is anything you don't understand, ask questions.

- To be sure you understood the other person accurately, paraphrase or recap what they said.

- Refrain from multitasking while someone is speaking, such as checking your phone or sending an email.

- Recognize and respect the feelings of the other person; you may do this without endorsing them.

Empathic communication is a very effective strategy for improving worker morale and brand perception. Better relationships, mutual respect, understanding, and more fruitful dialogues may all result from it. Simply maintain an open mind and pay more attention to the sentiments and ideas of others. By keeping these pointers in mind, you can help everyone work in a more productive atmosphere and build trust.

"Leadership is about bringing certainty to the world of uncertainty."

\- Tony Robbins

CHAPTER 3

THE HUMAN CAPITAL: NURTURING
THE WORKFORCE

The workplace of today is no longer a fixed, one-size-fits-all setting. Today's employees want places that can adjust to their varied demands and workflows, flexibility, wellness, and cooperation. Businesses are embracing flexible workplace design, a concept that values adaptability and meets the ever-evolving needs of a modern workforce, to prosper in this dynamic environment.

Imagine:

- Hot-desking: A lively center full of bustle with calm areas dotted throughout for concentrated work. Depending on their daily responsibilities and preferences, employees select their workplace.

- Modular furniture: Teams may customize their workspace for certain projects or meetings with the help of movable walls and adjustable workstations. This increases worker engagement and productivity by fostering a sense of control and ownership.

- Agile meeting spaces: Spaces for flexible and collaborative meetings must be able to change as fast as ideas do. Erasable walls, movable furniture, and integrated technology offer the ideal setting for ideation sessions, team meetings, and spontaneous get-togethers.

Additionally, it goes beyond the actual area. Workplace technology is essential to creating a genuinely dynamic work environment.

- Tech-enabled cohesive experience: Developing a unified work environment is more crucial than before. It can be challenging to promote a sense of connection and teamwork when staff members are dispersed across several locations and time zones. But technology has the potential to close the divide and establish a more cohesive corporate culture.

- Smart building systems: Temperature control, noise cancellation, and intelligent lighting all combine to provide a flexible and healthy work environment that maximizes productivity and well-being while accommodating individual preferences.

In today's changing business environment, having an agile and flexible workplace is not only necessary, but also an opportunity. You know where to look if you want to increase engagement, productivity, and job happiness.

Perspectives And Aspirations of Employees

Organizations that put employee growth and development first do well in today's competitive and dynamic business environment. Currently, more is needed to see your employees' potential while you are employed. It's critical to encourage this potential's development and assist them in achieving their professional goals.

Acknowledging and assisting your staff members in their career goals is a considerate gesture and a calculated investment that may pay off handsomely for your business and your staff members. This post will provide information on the many advantages of encouraging your staff members' goals and the most effective approaches to help them advance in their careers.

Supporting Your Employees' Aspirations

Over the past few decades, there have been substantial changes to the business environment. An important aspect emerging from the quickly growing business ecosystem is the growing focus managers and employers have on helping their staff members fulfill their professional goals.

Professional aspirations are long-term goals and objectives related to a person's work path. These goals might be to develop abilities and skills to succeed in their chosen area or to work in a position that satisfies particular desires.

In the modern workplace, employees actively create objectives, describe career expectations, and formulate ambitions to achieve their professional goals. People know exactly what they want from their professions, and many are steadfastly committed to achieving these goals. Workers are voicing expectations and setting standards with their employers; one important thing that companies need to do is actively support their career goals.

It may be tempting for an employer to see their job as ensuring tasks are completed. However, nowadays, an employee's development yields many advantages for the organization. As a result, all employers ought to be dedicated to supporting the development of their workforce and helping them achieve their career objectives.

Encouraging your staff to pursue their career goals has many benefits beyond personal growth. It not only helps them become better versions of themselves, but it also has a significant and lasting impact on their entire development. At the same time, the business gains from increased productivity and engagement as workers, motivated by pursuing their career goals, contribute significantly to the company's success.

In this fast-paced era, it is critical to acknowledge and promote your staff members' career goals to create a work environment that benefits both the individual and the business.

Should You Support Your Employees' Career Aspirations?

Once again, The Great Resignation has highlighted issues many companies could underplay. As more and more workers in the continuously shrinking labor market search for better opportunities and career fulfillment, it is clear that employee ambitions have taken on great importance in the corporate sector.

Workers are now more aware of the importance of a fulfilling career. Getting whatever comes their way is no longer their exclusive goal. They are now interested in me as I am actively pursuing their goals. As a result, many workers seek employers that share their goals and provide them with the growth possibilities they require.

Thus, the initial advantage of encouraging your staff members' professional goals—loyalty—is gone. However, unconditional devotion is not the only advantage of encouraging your staff to pursue their goals. What the corporation can do for its employees is now more important to its success than what the employees can achieve. Ultimately, employees become more picky about the qualities they want in a workplace.

Several businesses have developed ways to draw in and hold on to top people to stay relevant in the employment market. They accomplish this by offering remarkable corporate cultures and work settings that foster employee development and support career goals. Investing in people helps businesses succeed, and as a result, these businesses are outperforming their competitors.

Benefits of supporting your employees' career aspirations

The days of workers being happy with a stable job and a clear career path are long gone. The modern worker is motivated by a desire to advance both personally and professionally, and they look for chances that fit with their long-term objectives.

It is not unusual to see workers in today's labor market looking for companies that will have a major impact on their professional development. It is natural for employers to question whether providing these workers with the assistance and growth opportunities they desire is in their best interest. Ultimately, how can you be certain that they aren't just utilizing you as a springboard to further their careers?

However, as several polls have shown, one of the finest and most advantageous things a company can and should do is to promote their employees' professional goals.

The following are some advantages of encouraging your staff to pursue their goals:

Attracting Top Talent

According to an American Staffing Association (ASA) report, 80% of working individuals in the United States believe that professional growth and training opportunities are crucial when choosing a new employment. According to reports, all generations share this opinion, with 79% of Baby Boomers, 79% of Gen X, 84% of millennials, and 70% of Gen Z concurring that they base their employment decisions on the availability of prospects for professional advancement.

Before choosing a new workplace, employees consider several factors. Competitive pay, psychological safety, paid and unpaid perks, a fantastic work-life balance, and a nice work environment built around an equally positive work culture are all things that employees naturally desire. However, they also see professional development as necessary when deciding where to work and how long to stay there.

An organization creates a strong work culture, employer brand, and brand identity for itself when it provides the opportunity for its people to develop and achieve their goals. This attracts talent in the employment market, particularly top talent, and it works like magic.

In an era where talent is very scarce and even harder to draw in, your success as an employer depends on making every effort to obtain a recruiting advantage over your rivals. To draw in the most qualified applicants, supporting their goals is a good idea.

Don't only sell hopes and promises, though. Start by developing a fantastic workplace culture that actively seeks out employee development. This will demonstrate to potential candidates that you genuinely care about advancing the professional goals of your staff members.

Retention

One of the biggest advantages of encouraging your staff to pursue their goals is increased employee retention. One of the most significant and costly issues many companys deal with is retention. The Bureau of Labor Statistics report states that the overall rate of turnover was 57.3%. According to reports, over half of the workers quit their positions in pursuit of something new in only that one year.

Employees leave a company for a variety of reasons. Employees may be requested to quit or be laid off for involuntary causes. Other times, though, workers decide to leave a company for different reasons, such as low income, a lack of recognition, or frequently, a lack of opportunities for advancement. According to a workplace poll, 94% of participants said they would stay with a company longer if it invested in their professional development.

At a time when replacing an employee may cost up to 33% of their income, a company has to take every precaution to guarantee that employee retention is strong. This will not only save the cost of replacing staff members, but it will also remove the need to spend time and money on the recruiting process.

Businesses provide their employees with the job stability and pleasure they desire by assisting them in achieving their professional goals. Workers will feel appreciated at work as they will be content and more involved there. Because of this, they won't feel the need to go for professional progression elsewhere, which will guarantee they stay with the organization.

Increased Motivation

When workers aren't given the chance to advance in their careers, motivation levels might drop. When workers witness coworkers accomplishing goals they hope to achieve or may eventually achieve, this may get worse.

Engagement and motivation are intrinsically related in the workplace. A highly motivated employee typically performs very well, becoming involved in their work and sometimes even offering to help out. Employees, however, will make any effort to survive when their drive wanes. They care about completing their duties precisely; they are not motivated to go above and beyond to produce exceptionally high-quality work or perform beyond the call of duty.

Furthermore, workers get disinterested in their occupations when they cannot pursue their professional ambitions or have no avenue through which to do so. Burnout, stress, and, ultimately, resignation may result from this. This is similar to a garden, where plants flourish when given the necessary care and attention. They will only grow if you do something else.

Giving staff members the assistance they require to accomplish their professional objectives is a value exchange that demonstrates to them that your investment in their development increases with their level of effort. As a result, they are motivated to work harder at their duties.

Increased Productivity

A defined professional trajectory generally corresponds with a definite career objective in many people. Most significantly, they frequently know how to maximize their productivity when provided with the necessary skills, training, and other tools to enable them to achieve the professional goals they have set for themselves.

Worker productivity is crucial to any business's expansion. It assists the company in achieving objectives, coming up with creative ideas, offering top-notch customer support, and eventually being successful.

By providing career-building chances, employers foster mutual benefits and values among their workforce. Employees who receive growth support from their employers are more productive at work. Employee productivity is positively impacted by this efficiency, which enables them to successfully apply the lessons they have learned from these development possibilities by using the company's operations as a training ground.

Increased Profitability

The financial success of the business is frequently the culmination of all the advantages of fostering employee ambition. A company committed to helping its people achieve their goals often has more revenue and profitability than its rivals, even if this may require time and investment in the staff.

Opportunities for growth and development encourage employee engagement at work. The organization is also able to achieve its vision and goals thanks to this increased participation. Employees may assist the company in reaching additional milestones, many of which may be devoted to the organization's profitability, by actively working toward its goals.

Employee satisfaction, engagement, and attention to their responsibilities inside the company will also increase. This will encourage staff to put in a lot of effort towards achieving the company's common objective or vision while minimizing costly turnover.

How you can support your employees' aspirations

There is no standard for how a business should assist its staff in realizing their goals. The reality that every employee is different and has different career goals puts this to the test further. The company's distinct culture, the goals and requirements of its employees, and the resources at hand should all be considered when developing a plan to assist staff in realizing their potential.

A corporation may create a growth-oriented atmosphere for its employees in several ways. Among these are a few of these:

1. **Take An Interest In Employee Careers**

    Demonstrate to your staff that you are interested in their career objectives. Set up frequent meetings so that everyone is aware of their objectives and there is continuous communication. This will assist you to determine the resources you need to provide to support them in achieving their goals and demonstrate your value for them.

    Collaborate with staff members to develop a career path that will enable you to achieve these objectives. Establish clear goals and benchmarks for achievement, gather the resources needed to get there, and follow up with staff members often to make sure the targets are being fulfilled. Maintaining a direct, honest, and open line of communication is crucial to helping to attain these objectives.

2. **Provide Training Opportunities**

    A worker's development requires regular, high-quality education, workshops, seminars, and training. It will be easier for employees to accomplish their goals with these possibilities. More significantly, these training sessions allow staff members to network and form friendships with individuals with similar aspirations. Provide training opportunities based on the goals of your staff. Depending on the available resources, these chances might be physical or virtual.

To meet their demands, encourage staff members to seek pertinent business courses and seminars actively. If funds allow, ask mentors to guide your staff members as they work toward their professional objectives. Give your staff a way to stay informed about developments in the larger sector. This will guarantee that students keep learning and apply what they have learned to real-world situations.

3. Encourage Mentoring And Job Shadowing

An excellent tool for encouraging a worker to pursue their goals actively is a mentor. Therefore, establishing official mentorship programs is, ,among the greatest approaches to assistingassisting a worker. Mentoring is more than just a useful onboarding technique. It's a fantastic approach to share expertise, give advice, and offer new insights on supporting workers in achieving their professional objectives.

4. Rotate Employee Roles

One of the finest learning resources you can provide for your staff is variety. Consider allowing workers to work in various skill-related roles that might accelerate their development. Doing this will give your staff members the chance to learn new things, get fresh perspectives, and improve their comprehension of the company. It also promotes rapport-building and communication, which helps establish a feeling of community at work.

Creating A Supportive Culture At Work

As an employer, it is not only the right thing to do but also the compassionate thing to support your employees' professional objectives. It's also a tactic with much to offer the organization and its members individually.

Assisting your staff members in realizing their professional goals may help with a variety of issues, including motivation, retention, productivity, and engagement. Additionally, it builds a strong employer brand that draws in top personnel and establishes the company as an employer of choice. Prioritizing your workers' career goals can open up opportunities and help you create a flourishing, profitable business.

"*Resources are not the problem, it is resourcefulness.*"

- Tony Robbins

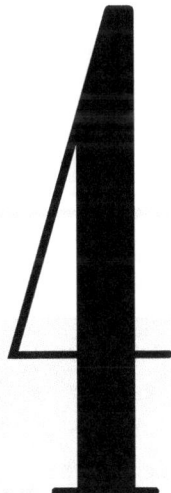

CHAPTER 4

LEADING BY EXAMPLE:
PERSONAL STORIES OF EMPATHY
IN ACTION

My heart would sink a little every time I walked the store floor. My team, usually a crackling fire of energy, felt…dampened. One of my team member I don't want to mention their name, a ray of sunshine on most days, seemed to be carrying the weight of the world. Numbers just weren't where they needed to be, and a heaviness clung to them like a fog.

Instead of barking about sales figures, a pit formed in my stomach. This wasn't about quotas; this was about them. So I took a deep breath and walked over, not to criticize, but to connect. "Hey," I started, placing a hand on their shoulder, "how are you?"

The dam broke. Tears welled in their eyes as they poured out their heart, a mix of personal struggles and work-related anxieties. At that moment, the numbers on the spreadsheet faded away. All that mattered was the person standing in front of me. Empathy became my compass. Forget targets, forget quotas. This was about helping someone I cared about weather a storm.

We talked for what felt like hours, crafting a plan not just for sales, but for them. It wasn't easy. There were setbacks and moments of doubt, but empathy was our guiding star. I became their cheerleader, their confidant, their rock. Slowly, a spark flickered back to life in their eyes. The numbers started to climb, but more importantly, so did their spirit.

Looking back, it wasn't the sales figures that mattered. It was the transformation I witnessed. It was the bond we forged through that shared journey. Empathy isn't a soft skill; it's the fire that ignites the best in ourselves and others. True leadership isn't about numbers on a page; it's about the impact we have on the lives we touch. And that, for me, is the greatest measure of success.

Help others achieve their dreams and you will achieve yours.

- Les Brown

CHAPTER 5

FROM BOARDROOM TO HOME:
EXTENDING EMPATHY BEYOND
THE OFFICE

Developing empathy outside of the workplace involves a broad range of interpersonal encounters and connections in addition to the formal workplace settings. In day-to-day interactions, empathy is essential for building comprehension, connection, and support. A caring ear to a buddy in need or a helping hand to a stranger are just two examples of how empathy actions performed outside the workplace greatly strengthen society.

Active listening is a crucial component of demonstrating empathy outside of the workplace. This entails paying attention to what others say and genuinely attempting to comprehend their feelings, viewpoints, and life experiences. By giving them our attention and responding with empathy, we provide a secure environment where they can freely and honestly express themselves. Empathic listening can reinforce bonds between people, foster trust, and provide much-needed solace in trying circumstances.

Kindness and assistance are vital ways to demonstrate empathy outside of the workplace. This may come in a variety of shapes and sizes, from providing helpful advice to giving consolation. Small acts of kindness, like lending a neighbor a hand with chores, supporting a friend through a breakup, or volunteering in the community, may profoundly impact someone's life. These deeds help the receiver and foster empathy and a feeling of community inside each of us.

Empathy also includes acknowledging and respecting other people's feelings outside the workplace. Even if we don't completely agree with someone's feelings, it's important to respect and validate their emotions. We may demonstrate to someone that their feelings are real and deserving of attention by accompanying their experiences. People can find great empowerment and accompanying in this validation, which gives them the confidence to deal with their feelings and difficulties healthily.

In addition, exhibiting empathy outside the workplace frequently means moving outside our comfort zones and admitting vulnerability. Sharing our challenges, experiences, and emotions may develop a greater sense of compassion and understanding between ourselves and others. We show that we're all human and in this together by being genuine and open about our path. This openness to vulnerability creates real relationships and fortifies the links of empathy in our communities.

Becoming empathetic and caring outside of the workplace is essential to contributing to society. We may build compassionate and understanding settings where everyone is seen, heard, and respected by practicing active listening, showing kindness, validating emotions, and embracing vulnerability. We make the world more compassionate and understanding by spreading empathy across professional lines.

The Principles of Mutual Respect

Building a cohesive and well-connected family structure starts with mutual respect. Trust and understanding flourish in a family when each member is treated with dignity and respect, which promotes harmony and togetherness. Recognizing and respecting each family member's uniqueness, beliefs, and boundaries is the first step in developing this mutual regard. Stronger familial ties result from a culture where everyone feels encouraged to express themselves honestly, and their opinions are valued.

Respect for one another in a family or at work means paying attention to what the other person says and accepting it even when disagreeing. Compromises may be achieved, and conflicts can be managed more skillfully when family members' points of view are shown empathy and understanding. The openness and collaboration fostered by this courteous communication are crucial for preserving the peace and closeness of the family.

Acknowledging and respecting one another's contributions, abilities, and skills is another essential component of mutual regard. Family members feel self-worth and belong when acknowledged and appreciated for their special talents and efforts. Recognizing one another promotes cooperation and support among family members as they work together to accomplish shared objectives, such as conquering obstacles or commemorating successes.

Furthermore, respecting boundaries and individuality within the framework is a part of mutual respect. Family members who respect one another's privacy, personal space, and individual decisions are likelier to feel trusted and independent. Respecting boundaries builds strong bonds based on acceptance and understanding, which paves the way for a peaceful home life where all members feel valued and protected.

Leading by example and introducing empathy, compassion, and tolerance in family relationships are necessary to promote mutual respect in a family or a business. Parents and other caregivers are essential role models when teaching kids the value of treating people with respect and compassion. Mutual respect may be prioritized in all facets of family life, including communication and decision-making, to help families build a solid bond and harmonious environment that will last over time.

The foundation stones for a balanced success are honesty, character, integrity, faith, love and loyalty.

- Zig Ziglar

DENTON GRAHAM

CHAPTER 6

BALANCING ACT: INTEGRATING
WORK AND FAMILY LIFE

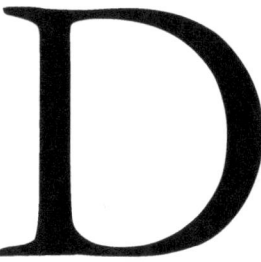**D**o you feel that work is all you do? You're not by yourself. According to several data, over 60% of American workers believe that their work-life balance is not in equilibrium. But with so much work being done at home, how can you manage your professional and personal lives? To be more productive, how do you manage your workload?

Is attending a yoga session once a week enough? Most importantly, how can you determine what works when the lines between work and home become increasingly hazy?

It might seem natural to feel overburdened and overworked since many struggle to balance their professional and personal lives. It need not be, though.

Why Work-Life Balance Is So Important

In addition to being beneficial for relationships and overall health, a healthy work-life balance may also raise employee productivity and performance. Your employees will work harder, make fewer mistakes, and be more likely to become brand ambassadors if they don't see their jobs as a chore.

Companies with a reputation for promoting work-life balance have grown increasingly appealing, particularly in light of the challenges associated with luring and keeping younger employees in this day and age. "Replacing an employee costs approximately $37,876 on average, and it takes up to 28 weeks to get them up to speed," according to Oxford Economics. Keeping your current staff content may be a smart strategy in light of this. By emphasizing work-life balance, you may increase retention rates and attract a valuable talent pool for new hires. It will guarantee a high caliber of internal talent while saving time and money.

Work-life balance is crucial for your employees and your company for the following additional reasons:

1. **Fewer Health Problems**

    Our physical and emotional health is at risk when we are overworked and under stress, endangering our social life.

Being overworked, exhausted, or stressed out will negatively impact our health. Having a poor work-life balance can cause several symptoms that are detrimental to our health. This includes anything from the common cold to life-threatening illnesses like strokes and breathing issues. White-collar professionals who worked three or more hours over what was necessary had a sixty percent increased risk of heart-related problems compared to those who did not work overtime, according to a UCL study involving over 10,000 participants.

Promoting self-care and finding equilibrium may drastically reduce health issues and absenteeism. This will guarantee that individuals desire to be a part of the business and culture and that your organization operates more efficiently during business hours.

2. More Engagement

You may boost employee engagement by assisting them in striking the ideal balance between work and personal life. This has a lot of advantageous effects: A global survey found that "operating income performance improved by nearly 52% in companies with highly engaged employees." Furthermore, "Organizations with high employee engagement increased their operating income by 19.2%, while organizations with low employee engagement saw a 32.7% decline in operating income."

When your employees are passionate about their work, they will go above and beyond for you and become devoted supporters of your company and merchandise. According to this poll, "engaged staff members are 2.5 times more likely to remain at work after regular business hours if there are tasks that need to be completed."

3. Fewer 'Burnouts'

Everybody experiences stress from time to time. It cannot be avoided. Workplace burnout may be prevented. Therefore, you should take steps to make sure your employees don't have one. When we feel overburdened and unable to keep up with obligations, we experience burnout. Every part of our lives can be negatively impacted by burnout. It is crucial to support your staff in taking time off and genuinely unwinding, as the inability to distinguish work from personal life will significantly raise the likelihood of burnout.

4. More Mindfulness

When we establish and maintain a good work-life balance, we have more control over our attention span and capacity to focus on the job. This is referred to as mindfulness. Wouldn't you prefer a team that is focused on what they are doing rather than worrying about work or home?

Your employees will be more committed to the task if you support them in striking a healthy work-life balance. Retention rates, output, and, eventually, profit will all increase.

What is an unhealthy work-life balance?

Achieving the ideal work-life balance can be challenging. There are moments when it appears like there is too much to accomplish, and we have pressing deadlines to meet, making work seem more important than our personal lives. However, working excessive hours can lead to burnout, stress, and neglect of your interests and interpersonal connections. Thus, keeping an eye on your well-being at work is critical. Take better care of yourself and your relationships with your loved ones in this way, which will reduce stress and help you keep good physical and emotional health. We will thus walk you through identifying the signs of a poor work-life balance:

1. You're always tired.

Excessive stress weakens the immune system and leads to physical ailments, making you more vulnerable to disease and exhaustion. Stress easily causes your body to ache and feel exhausted, putting your muscles and brain into "overdrive." Muscle pains, headaches that don't go away, dizziness, poor appetite, memory problems, depression, and lack of drive are all signs of stress. Aim to get at least 7-8 hours of sleep each day to revitalize your body and mind and begin increasing your self-care regimen.

2.   **You always work overtime.**

You must improve your time management if you spend more time at work than at home. While it's OK to stay late at work to complete chores for the day or even to get ahead for the next, doing so daily is not a desirable habit. Organizing and setting priorities for your daily duties will increase productivity and enable you to leave the office as soon as possible.

3.   **You bring your work home.**

University of Toronto research found that 50% of workers carry work home and that those who "hold professional jobs with more authority, decision-making latitude, pressure, and longer hours" are more likely to experience work-life interference. Work will continue to permeate your personal life if you are unable to control it. Remember to spend time with your loved ones and yourself after work. Work at home only when essential and only for brief periods.

4.   **You're getting out of shape.**

Have you noticed that you've gained weight lately? Your body is trying to advise you to get more exercise. Take a little stroll around your workspace as a break. Need more time to get to the gym? With the help of these fitness applications, you can still work out at home to reduce your body fat and track how many calories you consume.

5.   **You don't have time to enjoy yourself anymore.**

When did you last go on a trip with a buddy or see a movie at the theater? Overemphasizing work may cause you to miss enjoyable activities and priceless time spent with loved ones. Every week, make sure to engage in at least one pleasurable activity.

6. **You're struggling with your relationships.**

    Relationships suffer when there is an imbalance between work and life because people don't spend enough time together. You should reassess your goals and prioritize spending time with your loved ones if you cannot fit it into your schedule. Have a longer conversation with an old friend or around the dinner table. It helps us not only to decompress but also to remember to spend time with the people who are the real supporters of our lives. While business time may be made up, personal time and memories with loved ones cannot.

7. **You need to figure out what to prioritize.**

    Do you typically have too many undone tasks at the end of the day? This may indicate that you are taking on more work than you can handle. Establish priorities and concentrate on the things that matter. Develop your delegation skills if you are a manager. Give up attempting to handle everything on your own. Take on the most critical chores first and work your way down the list rather than trying to multitask and complete ten jobs simultaneously. Anything that cannot be achieved today can be completed tomorrow.

8. **You lose your patience way too easily.**

    Indeed, stress may make us tense. It's obvious when you need to take a break and step back when you become upset or agitated easily about small things. If you don't, pressure will eventually cause you to break. To teach your mind to concentrate on the positive, always see the silver lining in situations.

9. **Your personal space could be better.**

    You can only clean if you have time for yourself. Your house is now just a place to sleep and shower, and your workstation has become a mountain of paperwork. Burnout results from an overloaded brain in an untidy environment. Establish the routine of tidying your workstations at the end of each workday.

10. **You don't take a day off.**

   While dedication to one's profession is commendable, one's health should always come first. Utilize your sick and holiday leave when you need time to recover. To have the energy to face the problems ahead, try renewing your mind and body.

11. **You're always thinking of work**

   Even outside with loved ones, work is always on your mind or in your conversation. Recognize when to let go and take a quick break. It's admirable that you're actively pursuing your objectives, but remember that excess of anything is unhealthy. A balanced work-life schedule is essential for overall success.

Strategies And Techniques for Prioritizing Time - Work Life Balance

Pomodoro

Francesco Cirillo created the Pomodoro technique as a time management method. It divides your labor into intervals of 25 minutes, or "pomodoros," with five minutes of rest in between. It would help to take a 20-minute pause after each set of four pomodoros. The tomato-shaped kitchen timer Francesco used to monitor his progress gave rise to the name of this technique.

The Pomodoro technique is useful for planning and managing demanding jobs and projects. This tactic can aid in efficient planning and make it simple to track your development during each working session. This method will also help you control your stress, allowing you to take frequent pauses and unwind throughout the day. By using this technique, you can make sure that you are allocating enough time to all of the projects and objectives on your schedule and that work and play are balanced healthily.

Kanban

Kanban is a visual approach to time management that promotes organization and attention. Kanban, developed in the 1960s by Toyota Automotive's Taiichi Ohno, encourages efficiency and progress monitoring at every level of the manufacturing process. To enhance how activities flow across them, kanban groups jobs into columns or categories with labels for each stage. Thanks to this straightforward yet efficient solution, all parties involved are kept updated about all activities without requiring frequent progress checks.

To Do, Doing, QA (Quality Assurance), and Done, for instance, are the four columns of a standard setup, and all related tasks are monitored at every stage. This technique makes the overall state of the project clear and fosters better teamwork and communication by giving everyone in the team an easy-to-track mechanism that makes it clear who is working on what. The straightforward design of Kanban systems enables users to practice time management techniques, including goal-setting, planning, and more effective work delegation. Teams benefit from this method's increased visibility on individual tasks, which increases productivity.

Getting things done

David Allen developed the five-step "Getting Things Done" (GTD) approach to help manage and organize a lot of work as part of a productive system. Since its introduction in his book Getting Things Done: The Art of Stress-Free Productivity, managers, business owners, and students have embraced it. With GTD, you can rapidly turn your ideas into concrete tasks arranged in lists to ensure everything is remembered.

Planning and prioritizing daily tasks and time management will all be enhanced by using GTD successfully. After implementing the GTD technique, wanting to complete tasks more quickly and effectively is no longer just wishful thinking—it is now a realistic aim. Every stage of the process ensures that relevant action plans are in place in case something unexpected happens about finishing the initial work and recording the task itself. Whether you work from home or at school, GTD ensures everything on your to-do list gets done, giving you the peace of mind to concentrate on more important tasks.

Eat that frog

In his book Eat That Frog!, Brian Tracy introduced the time management strategy "eating the frog." 21 Amazing Ways to Finish More Tasks in Less Time and Quit Procrastinating. It motivates us to order our to-do list and start with the most crucial or challenging things. This entails choosing one work, sometimes called the "frog," for each day, starting on it early the next day, and giving it our whole focus before moving on to other duties.

This might be helpful to us since there are instances when we can find ourselves putting off these demanding, tedious, or unpleasant chores. Eating the frog is supposed to encourage us to do something challenging but crucial right now instead of putting off simpler but less vital tasks. We may increase our ability to plan, estimate, prioritize, be disciplined, and persevere by honing this time management skill, which will help us succeed.

Timeboxing

One time management strategy that both individuals and teams may utilize to accomplish their objectives is timeboxing. The concept is to set aside certain times ("timeboxes") for each activity, then complete the task within the allotted time frame before stopping. It is frequently employed in project management because it promotes set timelines and lessens the possibility of scope creep-related interruption.

In one of the chapters of his book Rapid Application Development, James Martin explained the idea more thoroughly. He stated, "In its most basic usage, a phase has a duration or length associated with it: a start date and an end date." Setting aside specified amounts of time for every job in your development strategy is known as timeboxing." If someone is interested in learning more about applying this strategy, several materials are accessible, including Timeboxing – The Complete Guide. Regular practice may assist in enhancing skills like anticipating delivery times and maintaining organization, which makes timeboxing a vital source management technique for anyone seeking to improve their managerial abilities and optimize productivity.

Time blocking

A well-liked and successful time management strategy is time blocking, which is making a timetable for oneself and blocking off specified periods to focus on a project or activity. It entails segmenting your tasks into manageable pieces and allocating time based on what suits you most. Elon Musk popularized this strategy by using it to balance his busy lifestyle.

By allowing you to set aside time for each work, time blocking can help you become more productive overall by removing the need for you to continually move between projects during the day, which can be highly distracting. Because you have to schedule how much time you will spend on each work, it also promotes efficient planning, which helps you stay organized and focused.

Since many people work from home these days, many new tools are available that can simplify time blocking, such as applications that allow you to plan activities straight from Google Calendar. Time blocking may help you become more focused and efficient, leading to considerably higher production. Think of time-blocking as an investment in yourself.

Inbox-zero

The foundation of the Inbox-Zero email inbox management strategy is keeping your inbox empty or almost empty. Efficiency guru Merlin Mann created it, encouraging users to prioritize their communication requirements, reduce email clutter, and single-task. This strategy aims to remove distractions so that it is simpler to recognize critical communications and promptly reply to emails that need attention.

The Inbox Zero strategy calls for filtering incoming emails, tagging specific communications as VIP so they can be found later, and, wherever feasible, unsubscribing from lists.

Process-smoothing techniques include assigning a time limit for replying to emails and classifying them according to significance. You can stay organized and never miss another crucial discussion by significantly lowering the amount of emails in your inbox.

Who's got the monkey

The 'Who's Got The Monkey?' method mainly targets project managers and how they can effectively handle their responsibilities. It alludes to the concept of assigning work while balancing time spent doing necessary duties as assigned by the supervisor, assisting coworkers with requests and inquiries, and taking initiative when faced with a challenge.

This approach uses the metaphor that all tasks are like monkeys, which you must balance to make the most use of the resources at hand.

This method refers to three kinds of monkeys: Boss-imposed time, System-imposed time, and Self-imposed time. Boss-imposed time is time spent on tasks mandated by one's superior; system-imposed time includes team or pack demands.

Last, self-imposed time refers to decisions a person makes for himself. Each of the three has a part in allocating resources to jobs within a project to maximize efficiency. In the end, it's critical to remember that, when used appropriately, Who's Got the Monkey may be a useful tool for project managers, giving them clarity when overseeing the workloads of their team members.

The eisenhower matrix

The Eisenhower Matrix is a well-liked time management method that bears the name of American President Dwight Eisenhower. To effectively prioritize activities, it classifies things as "important and urgent" or "not important and not urgent." Using this technique, you may evaluate activities based on their urgency and relevance, which will help you make a day plan and accomplish your objectives quickly.

Planning abilities may be enhanced by applying the Eisenhower Matrix approach for time management. It assists you in coming up with suggestions for how, given the work at hand, to make the most use of the available time. Another way to get started is to group tasks based on their importance: important and urgent, important but not urgent, neither important nor urgent, and not important but urgent.

Those that fit into the latter two categories ought to be removed immediately since they will eventually need additional effort and take much longer to complete. The first three might be ranked according to significance to get work started in that sequence. The advice in this matrix is a fantastic method to increase output, complete tasks faster, and improve organization in how you handle your everyday obligations.

The 10-minute rule

The 10-minute Rule is a very successful time-management technique. It may be used for various activities, including reading books, working on projects, maintaining long-term objectives, and preparing for tests.

The idea is straightforward: you commit to working on a job for at least ten minutes before determining whether to finish it. This can assist with exam preparation, project planning, and breaking down larger tasks into manageable bits of labor.

This strategy promotes stress management by giving users a sense of control and reducing their fear of beginning difficult new jobs or projects. Focusing for this brief time also helps in single-tasking because the temptation to get distracted is lessened during these little periods.

The 10-Minute Rule helps people prioritize their jobs and allows them to devote as much or as little time to any one activity without feeling overburdened by the amount of work that still has to be done.

To-done list

A to-do list helps you stay organized and on top of your activities. It is an alternative method of making a list of what you need or wish to accomplish later on, known as "To-Do" items. Rather than enumerating all of your objectives or tasks you hope to complete before the deadline, you list everything you have already done and completed within that time frame. You may devise future strategies for making the most of your time by tracking what has already been done.

A well-organized to-do list also helps with time management since it necessitates careful preparation and enables users to prioritize their chores appropriately. Users may monitor their progress daily and see that they are making significant progress toward reaching their larger-picture objectives, which helps reduce stress. It also resolves any problem with inefficient scheduling since, rather than depending only on guesswork to manage all that has to be finished on time, one would be actively involved with where they stand.

To-don't list

The To-Don't List is a creative method of time management and scheduling that offers a valuable alternative to the conventional To-Do List. One may more effectively organize their chores and activities with this strong tool. The To-Don't list encourages its users to enumerate duties and activities that may be safely set aside or neglected for the time being instead of setting down the things they wish to accomplish. When such behavior is considered, it enhances the ability to plan well by providing enough time between important commitments. Better stress management also results when life is too much to handle due to competing responsibilities.

The To-Don't List is also intended to assist in resolving scheduling conflicts, which frequently afflict those who find it difficult to plan their lives. Finding the time or motivation necessary to finish everything on their plate can be challenging without something like this available as an organizational tool. However, having a clear understanding of what needs to be done and what doesn't can provide a better perspective, giving them the necessary push. Over time, this will result in better time management abilities, which are incredibly helpful for daily living and work output.

Flowtime technique

The Flowtime Technique is an adaptable and cutting-edge method of increasing productivity. It was created in 2015 by software developer Dionatan Moura and adheres to sensible guidelines for working and rest periods. When using this approach, you allocate a certain period, usually between 10 and 90 minutes, for work-only work. You choose whether or not to continue working after the timer goes off. Flowtime enables users to have uninterrupted periods of concentration within their timeframe, in contrast to the Pomodoro Technique, which also relies on scheduled intervals, and Timeboxing, which forces users to stop when the timer goes off.

Although sessions last around an hour, you may use this job management technique whenever it works best for you. It can assist you in being more self-aware: When do I run out of steam? Which sort of deadline suits me the best? How frequently ought I to take pauses? Rather than forcing individuals to stick to tight time intervals, which can be challenging for some, this strategy promotes constructive flow. People may embrace creativity and responsiveness and match their activities with their rate of work and focus by using the Flowtime Technique.

Pareto analysis

The Pareto Analysis also called the 80/20 rule, is a time management principle that Vilfredo Pareto, an Italian economist, initially formulated. Its underlying theory holds that 80% of results are determined by 20% of an individual's activities. Using this technique, one may determine the major life activities that provide the highest return on intended results. You may achieve up to 80% of your goals and objectives by concentrating on this 20% of the total.

The Pareto Analysis advises us to properly prioritize our tasks and concentrate on our areas of interest regarding time management. To do this, it's critical to identify the genuinely worthwhile activities and formulate an action plan around those yielding the highest return. This method simplifies gradually removing obstacles or rocks to advance more. Additionally, the procedure offers busy professionals a practical means of maintaining productivity and practicing time management.

1-3-5 rule

Using the 1-3-5 Rule to organize your chores is a good idea. Its basic idea is to dedicate one large task, three medium-sized activities, and five little chores to your attention each workday. Prioritizing one large work at a time will make you feel accomplished and inspired to keep going. Break down the three medium jobs into smaller projects so you can move forward without being bogged down by a big project. The five smaller activities help divide bigger jobs into manageable portions and are useful for preventing procrastination.

This approach can assist with work prioritization and attention by ensuring that the most critical activities are completed before moving on to more relaxed goals. It also permits flexibility, as it is simple to rearrange the day's objectives to consider unforeseen circumstances. Furthermore, it promotes delegation since it allows the user to select which tasks are their responsibility and which may be assigned to others. Ultimately, following this guideline guarantees efficiency and production while reducing stress by juggling several responsibilities simultaneously.

Abcde method

The ABCDE Method is a straightforward yet powerful method for planning tasks. It was created by Alan Lakein and is included in his book How to Get Control of Your Time and Your Life. By using this technique, individuals can improve their ability to prioritize and finish their chores ahead of schedule. In contrast to the Eisenhower Matrix, the ABCDE approach assists people in setting priorities and assigning time-sensitive jobs appropriately. It achieves this without simply classifying tasks based on urgency.

Using this system, tasks are ranked from A to E according to priority, with "A" representing the most crucial work that must be finished first and "E" representing less urgent duties. In this manner, customers can rapidly review their daily tasks and immediately take on the most important ones. The ABCDE technique also restores power to those who feel helpless or overburdened by everyday responsibilities. Just concentrate on the most pressing tasks, and they will be completed. No task requires full concentration for a lengthy amount of time!

Posec method

Steve Lam created the POSEC technique, a novel approach to time management. This approach contends that to manage a hectic schedule effectively; one must divide one's long-term objectives into manageable chunks and rank them in order of importance. The process begins with ranking critical tasks according to their urgency and importance, sorting them into priority order to complete the most critical ones, optimizing workflow to reduce steps, and conserving resources by avoiding wasting time or effort on unrelated activities.

The POSEC approach has the benefit of effectively allocating users' resources while directing them toward meeting predetermined goals within a predetermined window of time. Along with increasing awareness of everyday activities, this systematic approach gives people insight into improving their processes for higher production. Those who have used this practice have reported increased attention and work completion, which frequently results in increased productivity and enhanced time management abilities.

Pickle jar theory

An efficient method for allocating your time and duties so that you may concentrate on the most crucial job is the Pickle Jar Theory. It is based on putting different items inside a jar, such as sand, pebbles, twigs, and stones. You may prioritize your tasks and ensure care of your most critical functions by seeing how each job fills the jar.

Utilizing this approach calls for extensive goal-setting and preparation. It would help if you decided which jobs are necessary, which ones may be completely removed, and which ones can be assigned to someone else. The main advantage of applying the Pickle Jar Theory to your calendar is that it makes distinguishing between worthwhile and pointless jobs easier. By carefully organizing your schedule, you may free up some space in your daily routine and improve time management by concentrating on what's truly important.

In the end, time management is a personal choice. The ability to manage your time well is a talent that requires practice and commitment. Do we work hard enough to accomplish our most significant and worthwhile goals? Do we give ourselves enough time to unwind and rest? A little reflection on these issues can improve our time management skills and point us toward increased personal fulfillment. However, you may immediately improve your productivity and organization with the methods and approaches covered in this book section.

You may achieve more performance while balancing your personal interests and professional objectives by making your schedule and paying attention to how you spend your time. It's simpler than ever to reach optimum efficiency at work or school thanks to the abundance of tools and techniques accessible. When applied correctly, these techniques can assist people in maintaining their attention on tasks while enabling them to enjoy their leisure activities.

I'm not the smartest. But you will not outwork me! I wake up every morning at 3 o'clock!

\- Eric Thomas

CHAPTER 7

THE RIPPLE EFFECT: EMPATHY AS
A CATALYST FOR CHANGE

In a society where negativity and conflict are common, kindness stands out as a force for hope and may spark profound change. It is more than just a soft virtue confined to the periphery of human contact; it can transform societies, spur social movements, and mend broken relationships. Let's examine why kindness is essential for bringing about constructive social change rather than only being a polite phrase.

Kindness is fundamentally the global language of compassion, empathy, and understanding. It creates ties that unite us as a global society by bridging ethnic, cultural, and ideological divides. By showing kindness to others, whether via a smile, a helping hand, or a kind deed, we reinforce our commitment to support one another and our common humanity.

The ripple effect of compassion is among its most significant features. Acts of kindness radiate outward, impacting lives much beyond the immediate encounter, like a stone thrown into a pond. A small deed of kindness may start a chain reaction spreading throughout communities and beyond national boundaries. Kindness may spark a grassroots movement for good change by bringing people together around a shared goal and inspiring group action.

Being kind may change a person—the giver and the recipient. Several studies have demonstrated that deeds of kindness improve the mental and emotional wellbeing of the donor as well as the welfare of the recipients. Acts of kindness cause our brains to release oxytocin, sometimes known as the "love hormone," which lowers stress and increases emotions of happiness. Therefore, by acting kindly toward others, we improve their well-being wellbeing ide our lives, a feeling of fulfillment and purpose.

Kindness also acts as a potent counterbalance to the dominant culture of hate and separation. Being polite to those we disagree with can help to heal divisions and promote communication in a society full of polarization and conflict. We provide room for understanding and healing when we address disagreements with empathy and respect instead of hate and disdain. In this sense, kindness acts as a catalyst for bridging gaps and promoting an inclusive and cooperative society.

Kindness is the foundation of a vibrant civil society on a social level. Communities that value empathy and compassion are better able to withstand hardship. Kindness builds social ties, a feeling of community, and support networks that improve the population's wellbeing. In addition, acts of kindness encourage people to work together to confront structural inequalities and urgent social challenges by uniting people to assist the weakest members of society and push for change.

Being kind is more than just a passing gesture; it can be a powerful force for good in society. Its repercussions extend beyond personal encounters, influencing the structure of our societies and the course of history.

Let us remember that kindness is a necessity rather than a luxury as we negotiate the complexity of the modern world. Kindness is a guiding concept that can heal, unite people, and improve the world. Therefore, let's all do our modest part to spread kindness wherever we go, knowing that when we work together, we can build a future characterized by empathy, compassion, and respect for one another.

How To Harness The Power Of The Ripple Effect

How can you use the ripple effect, now that you know its potential, to improve both your life and the environment around you?

- Start small: Pay attention to the impact of tiny adjustments. Every adventure starts with a single step, just as every large wave begins with a little ripple. Build with a simple, easy-to-implement minor adjustment at first.

- Focus on habits: Habits are the foundation of the ripple effect. A positive habit you form, such as daily exercise or meditation, might set off a series of beneficial events that will resonate throughout your life.

- Be intentional: You must be deliberate in your activities if you want to cause a ripple effect. Consider the impact you wish to produce, then take steps toward achieving that effect.

- Pay it forward: The impact spreads easily. Making good changes in your own life might encourage others to follow suit. Please share your improvements with others and inspire them to create their ripples to pay it forward.

A potent idea that serves as a reminder that even seemingly insignificant actions may have a significant influence is the ripple effect. You may make a big difference in your life and the world by beginning small, concentrating on habits, being purposeful, and giving back. So go ahead and make that tiny adjustment; you never know what kind of ripple effect it may have.

How Fostering Empathy Can Drive Positive Social Change

Developing empathy is vital for bringing about constructive societal change, not just a personal quality. Understanding and sharing another person's emotions, or having empathy, may profoundly impact society by fostering compassion, understanding, and teamwork. Empathy training helps people and communities become more sensitive to the needs, difficulties, and experiences of others. This understanding may be used to take meaningful action addressing social problems and advancing justice and equality.

First, encouraging empathy helps individuals from different backgrounds feel connected and supportive of one another. Through acknowledging and comprehending the viewpoints and experiences of others, people may dismantle obstacles related to bias, discrimination, and prejudice. This feeling of unity creates a collective identity that surpasses differences and encourages cooperation and teamwork in the pursuit of shared objectives. In this sense, empathy promotes societal cohesiveness and togetherness by acting as a link between individuals.

Second, empathy fosters a culture of kindness and compassion by motivating selfless deeds. This leads to constructive societal transformation. People are more inclined to do deeds of mercy, charity, and assistance when empathizing with the less fortunate or oppressed. Acts of kindness, whether they take the form of helping at a nearby shelter, standing up for the rights of underrepresented groups, or listening to someone in need, can have a positive knock-on impact that uplifts entire communities and promotes an environment of compassion and empathy.

By influencing lobbying efforts and decision-making processes, cultivating empathy helps people become more effective change agents. Policymakers, leaders, and activists who address social challenges with empathy learn more about these crises' intricacies and underlying causes. This knowledge makes it possible to provide more thoughtful and compassionate solutions that consider the wants and requirements of all parties involved and provide more fair and long-lasting results.

In the face of disagreement and hardship, empathy promotes resiliency and forgiveness. People and groups may handle differences and conflicts with compassion and understanding instead of hate and division by cultivating empathy. Building bridges of understanding and reconciliation and peacefully resolving problems depend on one's capacity to empathize with others' viewpoints and experiences. In cultures ripped apart by division and violence, empathy functions as a potent instrument for mending wounds, establishing trust, and promoting peace and reconciliation.

Encouraging empathy is critical to bringing about constructive social change because it fosters compassion, understanding, and collaboration between people and communities. Through developing empathy, individuals may bridge gaps, motivate selfless deeds, support advocacy initiatives, encourage healing and resilience, and eventually create a more equitable, inclusive, and compassionate society. We can leverage empathy's transforming ability to make the world a better place for everyone if we encourage empathy in ourselves and others.

"You have to understand your own personal DNA. Don't do things because I do them or Steve Jobs or Mark Cuban tried it. You need to know your personal brand and stay true to it."

\- Gary Vaynerchuk

CHAPTER 8

THE JOURNEY AHEAD: EMBRACING
CONTINUOUS IMPROVEMENT

Michelle Obama once said, "Being for me isn't about arriving somewhere or achieving a certain aim." Instead, I view it as a way to go forward, change, and always strive to become a better version of myself. The voyage never ends. The principle of constant self-improvement is succinctly expressed in this potent remark.

Indeed, the road to self-improvement never ends. It inspires us to become better versions of ourselves and promotes personal progress. Every step we take on the path to self-improvement gets us one step closer to realizing our objectives and improving our lives.

Professional development is likewise predicated on self-improvement. It motivates us to continuously pick up new talents, improve our abilities, and raise our workplace worth. This dedication to lifelong learning fosters professional growth and creates doors to new prospects.

Because the world is always changing, we must be able to adapt. Constant self-improvement gives us the flexibility to adapt to these changes and keeps us open to fresh concepts and methods of doing things. In this way, self-improvement guarantees that we not only survive but also prosper under a variety of conditions.

Additionally, enhancing oneself leads to a feeling of contentment. The sense of fulfillment that comes from always pushing forward and trying to be better gives our life meaning and a strong sense of accomplishment. Our duty as subject matter experts and influencers is to exemplify the transformational potential of ongoing self-improvement. By sharing our personal development and evolution stories, we may encourage others to start along the path of self-improvement.

In the end, Michelle Obama's remarks are a powerful reminder of the significance of this never-ending quest for improvement. The trip itself—the unwavering pursuit of fulfillment, flexibility, and personal and professional growth—is more important than the final destination. Together, let's embrace the path of ongoing self-improvement, motivate people through our stories, and build a society full of development opportunities.

The Role of Continuous Improvement In Business Success

Long-term business success is contingent upon continuous development. Organizations may cultivate an atmosphere where workers are empowered to propose and execute changes by promoting a culture of learning and innovation. Employee happiness, loyalty, and a sense of accountability all rise due to this involvement.

Additionally, due to constant development, businesses can adjust to shifting consumer tastes and market situations. It guarantees that businesses meet or exceed customers' expectations and helps them remain relevant. Companies may increase profitability by minimizing waste and optimizing efficiency via continuous process monitoring and adjustment.

Continuous improvement's effect on the advancement and development of employees is another facet. Organizations may foster a culture of constant learning by empowering staff members to take responsibility for their work and participate in the development process. This improves each person's abilities and expertise while fortifying the company.

An effective mentality that propels corporate success is continuous improvement. By adopting this concept, businesses may improve their procedures, goods, and services, boosting client happiness and operational effectiveness and providing a competitive advantage in the marketplace.

Case Studies of Successful Continuous Improvement

After discussing the methods for putting continuous improvement into practice, let's look at a few case studies showing how these methods have succeeded.

Google's Culture of Innovation

Another business that has grown by placing a high priority on ongoing development is Google. Employees are encouraged to think creatively, take calculated chances, and consistently question the status quo because of their innovative culture.

Google's well-known "20% time" policy, which permits staff members to dedicate a segment of their working hours to side projects, has produced ground-breaking products like Gmail and Google News. By cultivating an environment that appreciates and promotes experimentation, Google consistently pushes the envelope of what is conceivable.

Intel's Copy Exactly! Methodology

Intel has achieved significant growth by prioritizing continuous improvement through its "Copy Exactly!" methodology. This approach mandates that every aspect of the semiconductor manufacturing process is standardized and precisely replicated across all Intel facilities worldwide. By ensuring uniformity, Intel can quickly implement any enhancements or innovations across its entire network. This meticulous attention to consistency not only improves efficiency and product reliability but also demonstrates empathy towards employees, customers, and partners by maintaining high standards and minimizing variability. Through this method, Intel continuously drives operational excellence and industry-leading advancements.

Overcoming Challenges in Continuous Improvement

Even if constant progress has many advantages, there are drawbacks. Organizations need to be ready to confront and overcome these challenges to guarantee that their improvement projects are successful.

Resistance to change

Resistance to change is one of the most frequent problems during projects for continuous improvement. Workers may oppose new policies, practices, or instruments because of concern that they may impact their positions or status.

Organizations must explain the rationale behind the enhancements and the advantages they will provide to overcome opposition to change. Open communication and transparency may allay fears and give workers a feeling of pride in their work.

Maintaining momentum in improvement efforts

Sustaining the improvement activities' momentum over time is another difficulty. Once initial gains are made, it is easy to grow comfortable or return to the old methods.

Organizations should aggressively celebrate and acknowledge accomplishments to keep people motivated and engaged. Furthermore, improvement projects should be periodically reviewed and revisited to guarantee that improvements are maintained and expanded upon. It takes a proactive attitude, a dedication to learning, and an openness to change to achieve continuous progress. Organizations may enhance their ability to continually adapt and develop, which is crucial for long-term success in today's ever-changing business landscape, by putting the techniques we've covered into practice.

Leadership's new must-have isn't a skill set; it's a heart set—where empathy takes center stage, shaping connections and driving progress."
- Denton Graham

CONCLUSION

While the benefits of empathic leadership are obvious, its implementation is not without problems. In a society dominated by measurements and outcomes, the intangible quality of empathy may be neglected or underestimated. However, the ultimate measure of leadership is not just in the bottom line, but also in the influence it has on hearts and minds.

As we conclude this book, let us remember the core of empathic leadership: a willingness to see beyond titles and responsibilities, a commitment to creating connection and understanding, and an appreciation for the fundamental humanity that binds us all. For in the tapestry of leadership, empathy is the thread that connects us all, creating a story of compassion, resilience, and common purpose.

ACKNOWLEDGMENTS

I am grateful for the support and collaboration of those who contributed to the creation of this book. Their assistance was invaluable in bringing this project to completion.

Do Not Go Yet; One Last Thing To Do

If you liked this book or found it useful, I'd appreciate it if you could leave a quick review on Amazon. Your support is greatly appreciated, and I personally read all of the reviews in order to obtain your feedback and improve the book.

Thanks for your help and support

!